BOOK 2

Grand DUETS FOR *Christmas*

8 ELEMENTARY ARRANGEMENTS FOR ONE PIANO, FOUR HANDS

Melody Bober

Christmas is a joyous time of year filled with events that create a lifetime of memories. I remember the huge Christmas tree at my grandparents' house, homemade holiday treats, the reading of the Christmas story from the Bible, and, of course, Santa's visit! Christmas music was always the highlight for me and truly captured the spirit of the season.

In that spirit, I have written *Grand Duets for Christmas, Book 2* to provide memorable experiences for today's students at the piano. Whether performing with a teacher, sibling, parent, or friend, students can learn familiar Christmas music that will help them progress technically and musically. Rhythm, phrasing, articulation, and dynamics all become wonderful teaching tools while students listen for the unique blending of the two parts.

Duets continue to spark excitement in my studio. I sincerely hope that you will enjoy using these *Grand Duets for Christmas* this holiday season!

Best wishes,

CONTENTS

Alfred Music
P.O. Box 10003
Van Nuys, CA 91410-0003
alfred.com

ISBN-10: 1-4706-4064-3
ISBN-13: 978-1-4706-4064-4

Cover Photos
Christmas tree 1: © Getty Images / YinYang • Christmas tree 2: © Getty Images / diegograndi • Christmas tree in foreground: © Getty Images / Lloret •
Holiday decorations: © Getty Images / ArtBoyMB • Christmas lights: © Getty Images / MentlaStore • Village: © Getty Images / Rastan

O Come, All Ye Faithful

Secondo

John Francis Wade
Arr. Melody Bober

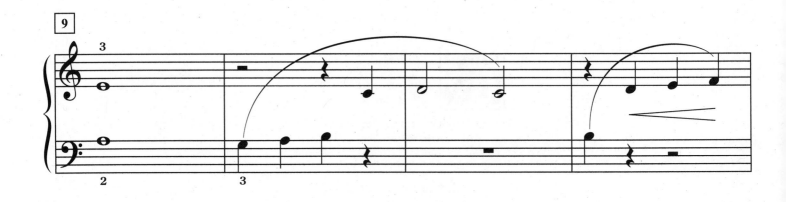

O Come, All Ye Faithful

Primo

John Francis Wade
Arr. Melody Bober

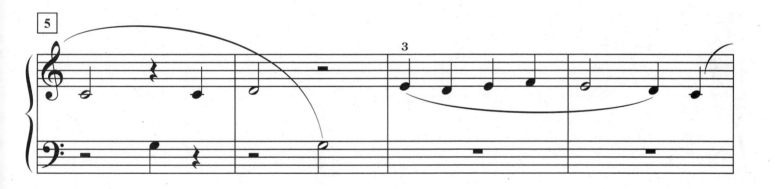

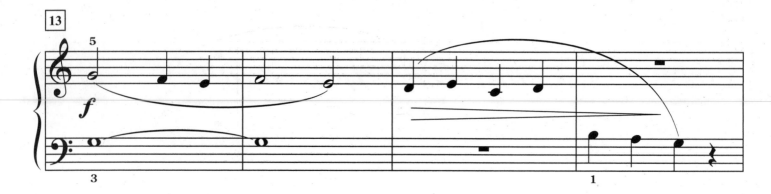

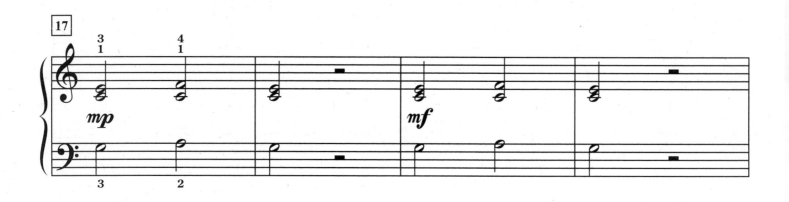

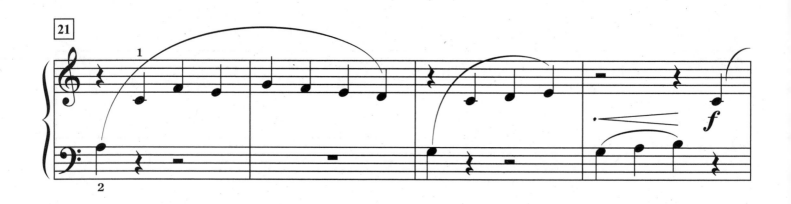

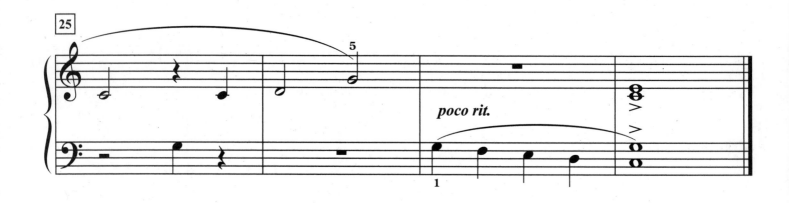

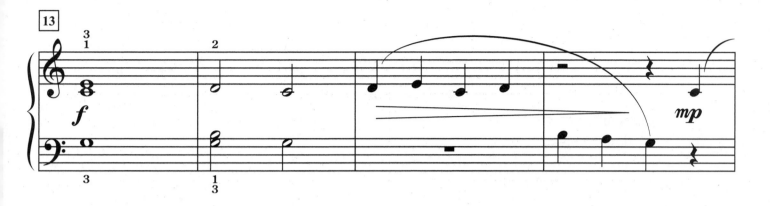

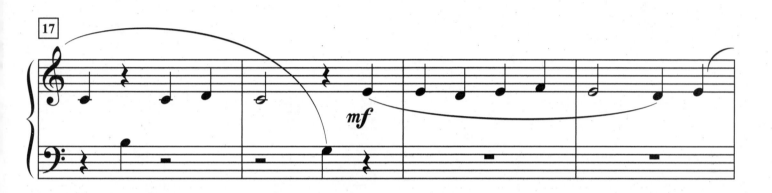

Away in a Manger

Secondo

James R. Murray
Arr. Melody Bober

Peacefully (♩ = 116)
Both hands one octave lower throughout

Away in a Manger

Primo

James R. Murray
Arr. Melody Bober

Peacefully (♩ = 116)

Both hands one octave higher throughout

O Come, Little Children

Secondo

Johann A. P. Schulz
Arr. Melody Bober

O Come, Little Children

Primo

Johann A. P. Schulz
Arr. Melody Bober

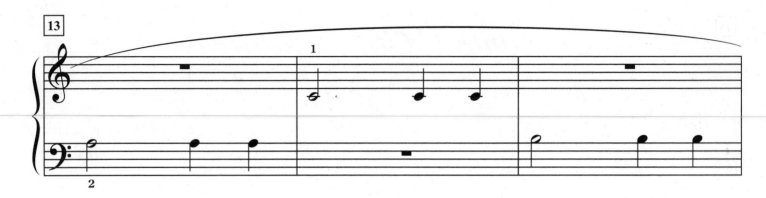

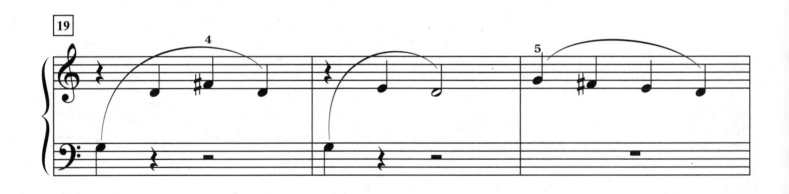

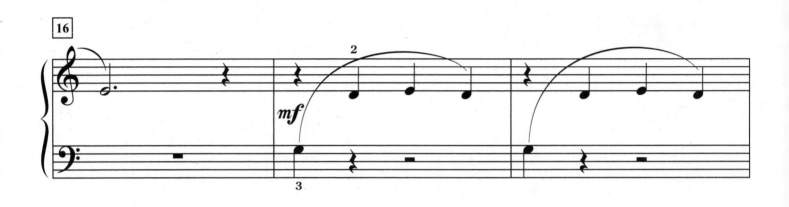

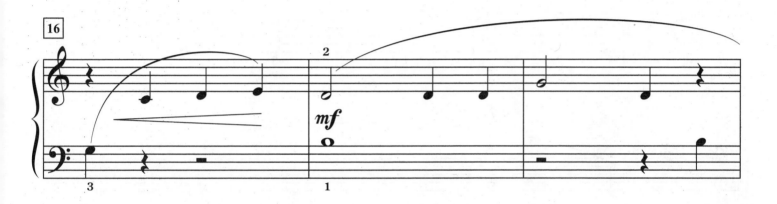

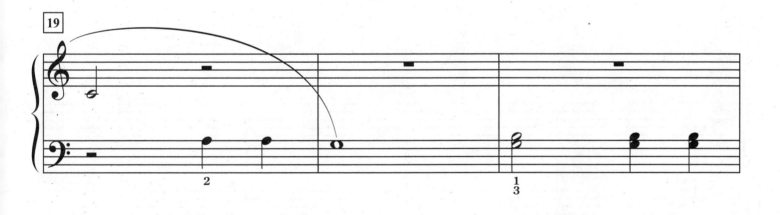

Up on the Housetop

Secondo

Benjamin R. Hanby
Arr. Melody Bober

Animated (♩ = 120)
Both hands one octave lower throughout

Up on the Housetop

Primo

Benjamin R. Hanby
Arr. Melody Bober

Animated (♩ = 120)
Both hands one octave higher throughout

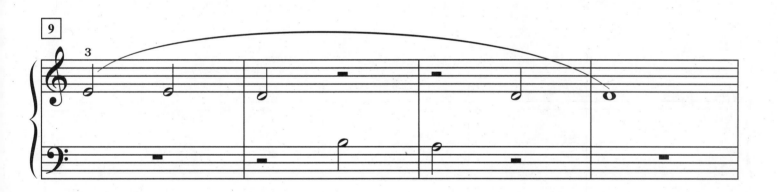

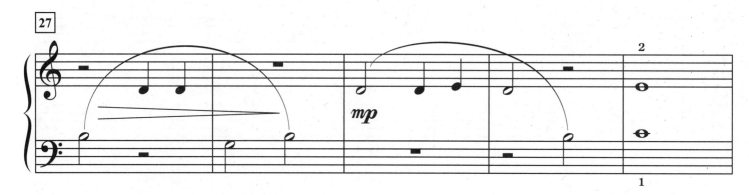

Rise Up, Shepherd, and Follow

Secondo

Spiritual
Arr. Melody Bober

Rise Up, Shepherd, and Follow

Primo

Spiritual
Arr. Melody Bober

With energy (♩ = 88)
Both hands one octave higher throughout

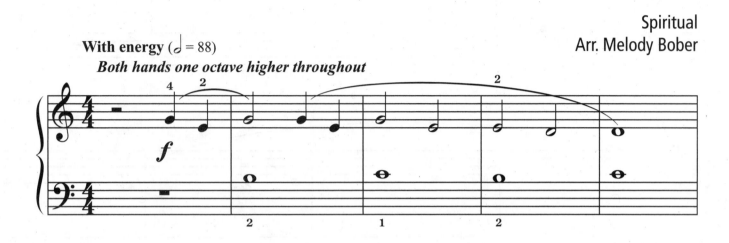

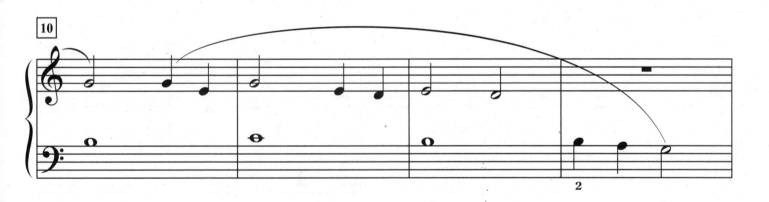

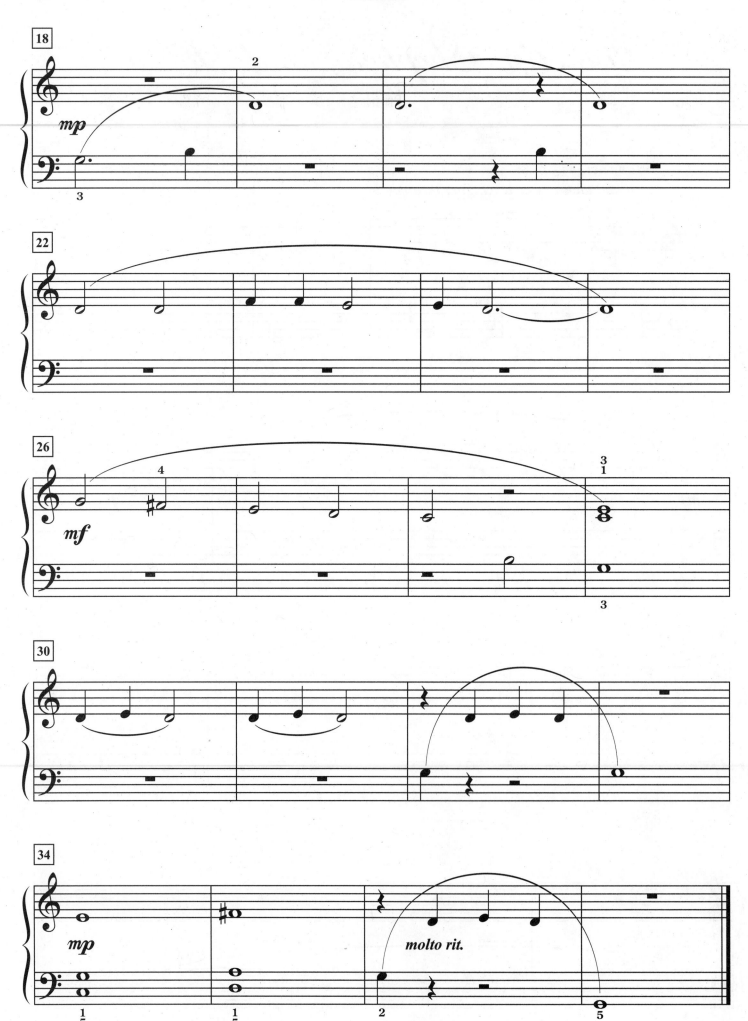

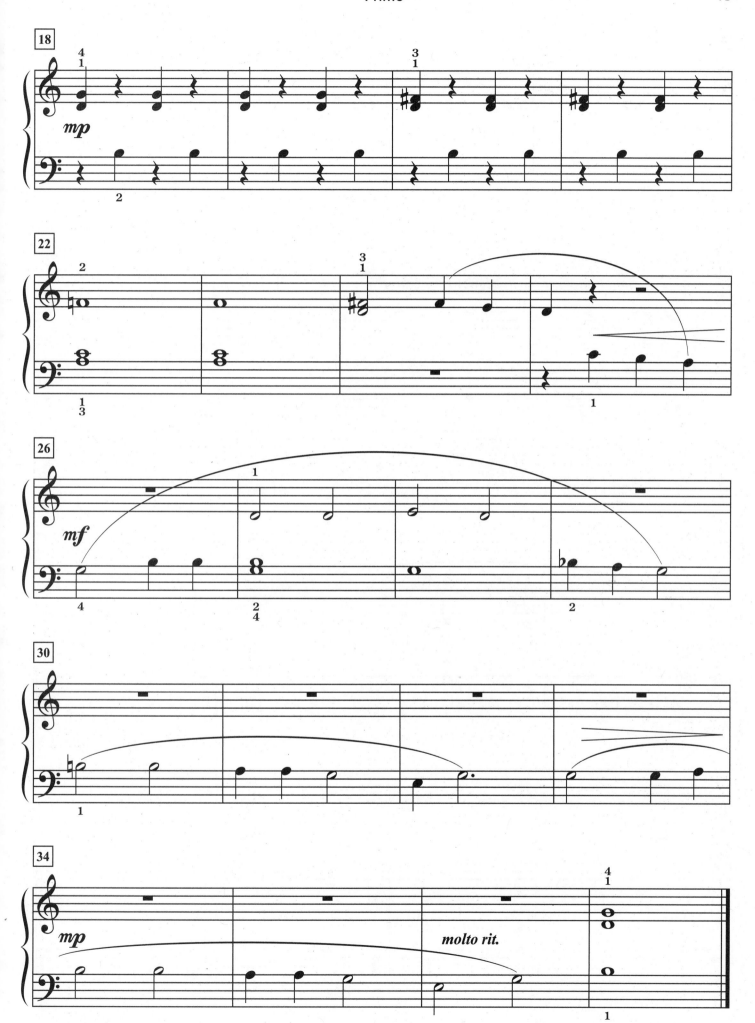

O Come, O Come Emmanuel

Secondo

Plainsong
Arr. Melody Bober

Expressively (♩ = 108)

Both hands one octave lower throughout

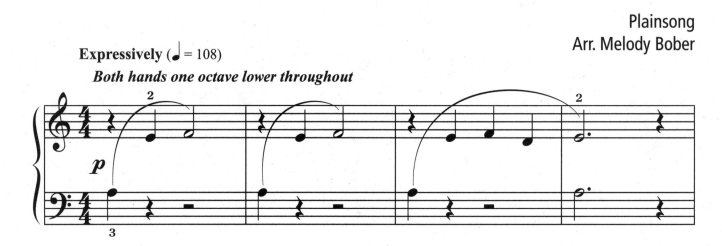

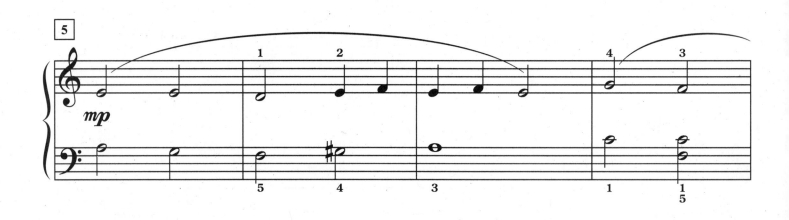

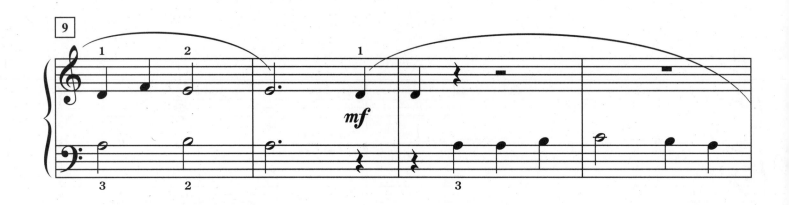

O Come, O Come Emmanuel

Primo

Plainsong
Arr. Melody Bober

Expressively (♩ = 108)
Both hands one octave higher throughout

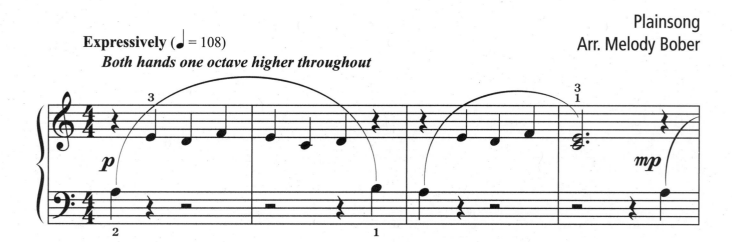

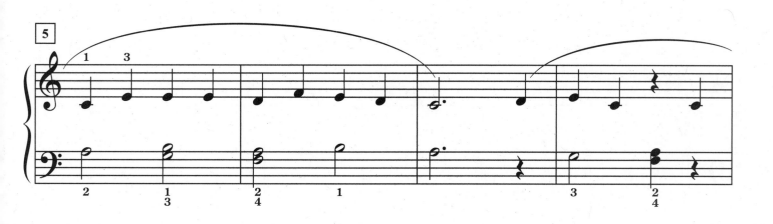

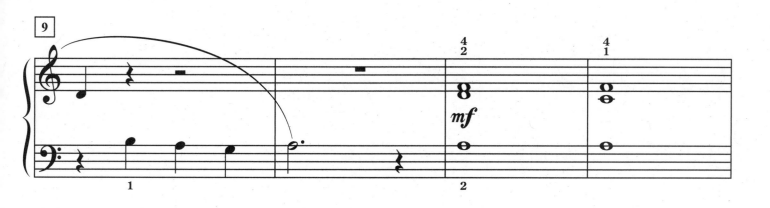

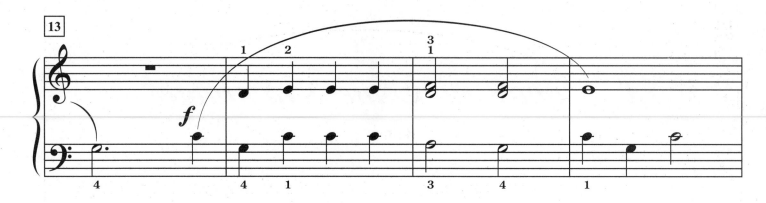

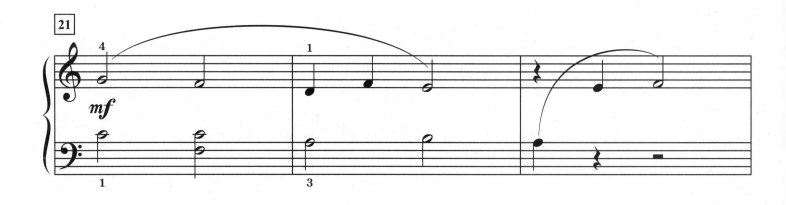

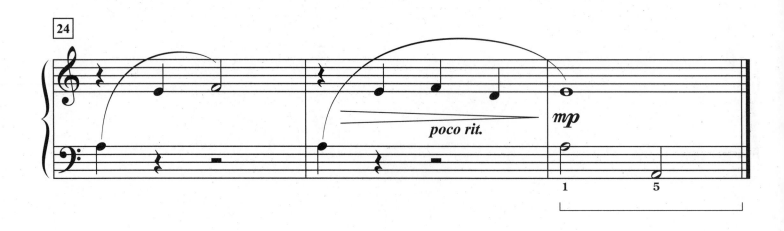

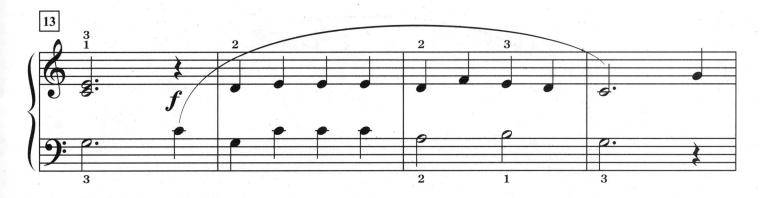

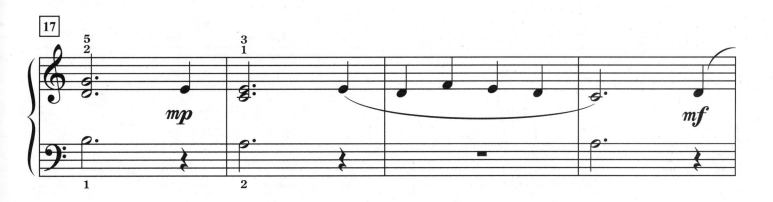

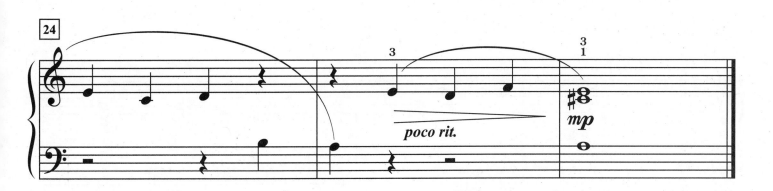

Good King Wenceslas

Secondo

Traditional
Arr. Melody Bober

Good King Wenceslas

Primo

Traditional
Arr. Melody Bober

Secondo

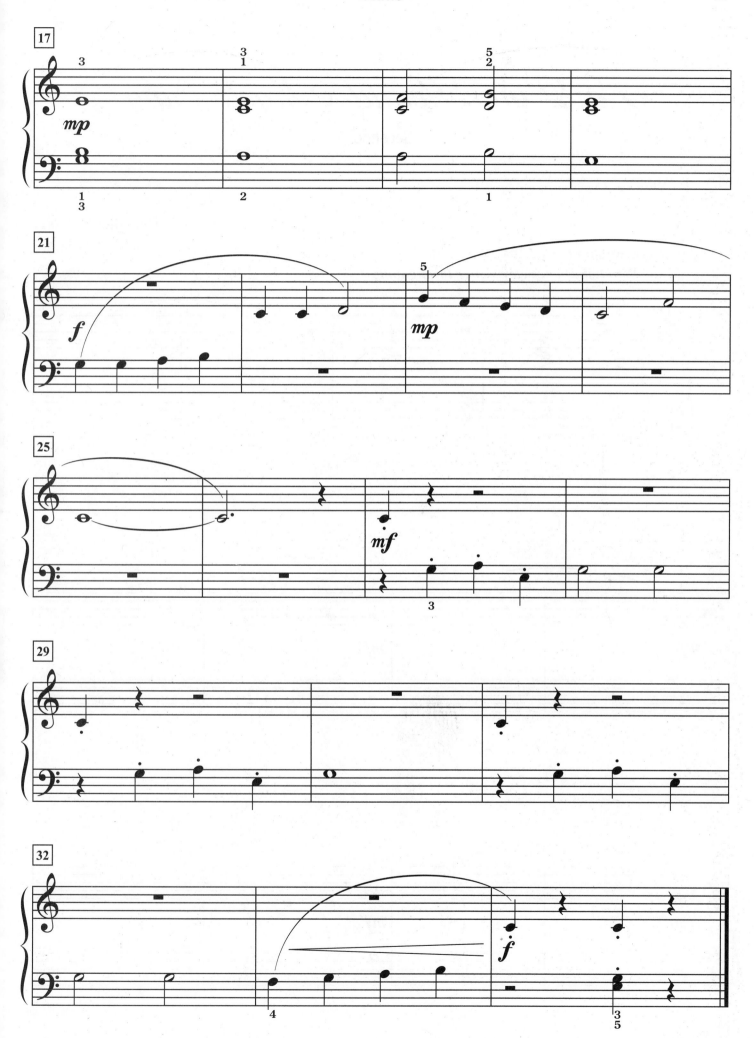

Hark! the Herald Angels Sing

Secondo

Felix Mendelssohn
Arr. Melody Bober

Triumphantly (♩ = 144)
Both hands one octave lower throughout

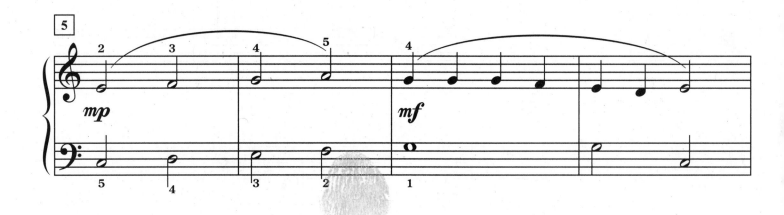

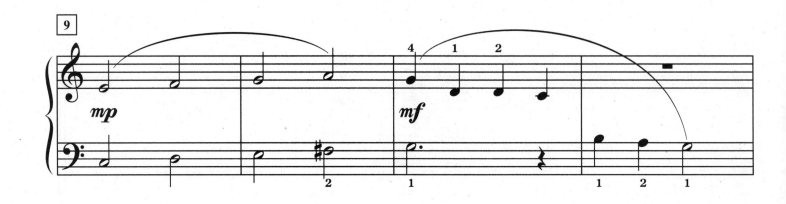

Hark! the Herald Angels Sing

Primo

Felix Mendelssohn
Arr. Melody Bober

Triumphantly (♩ = 144)

Both hands one octave higher throughout

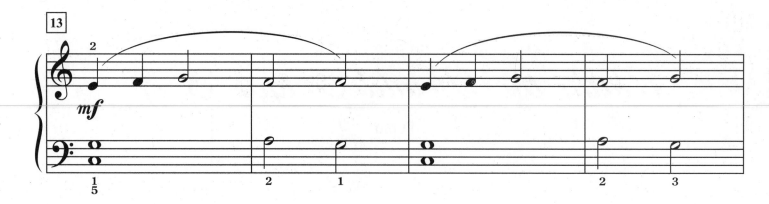

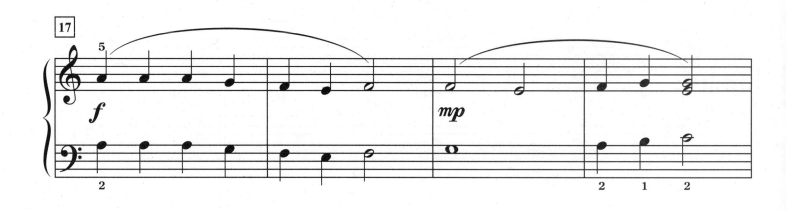

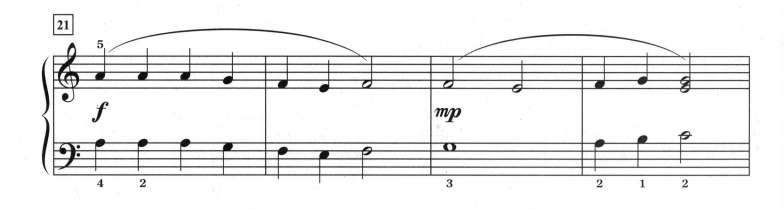

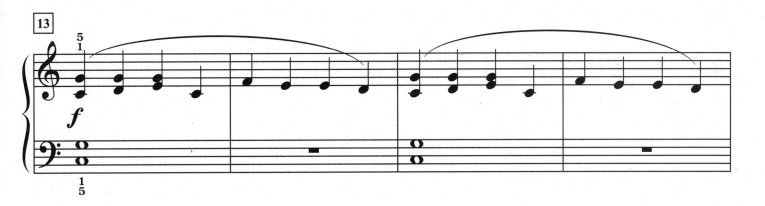

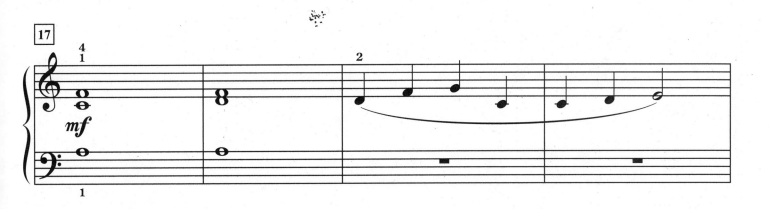

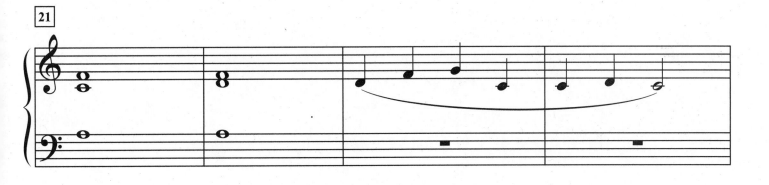

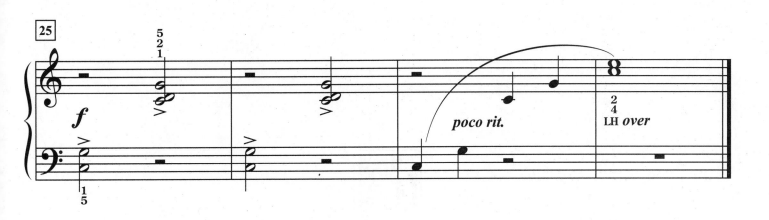